PEOPLE AND NEIGHBORHOODS

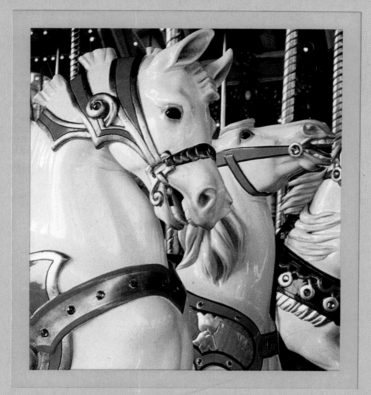

Everyone has fun riding the merry-go-round in a neighborhood park.
A park is just one of the special places in a neighborhood. What do
you like best about your neighborhood?

BARRY K. BEYER

JEAN CRAVEN

MARY A. McFARLAND

WALTER C. PARKER

MACMILLAN/McGRAW-HILL SCHOOL PUBLISHING COMPANY
NEW YORK   CHICAGO   COLUMBUS

PROGRAM AUTHORS

Dr. Barry Beyer
Professor of Education and American Studies
George Mason University
Fairfax, Virginia

Jean Craven
Social Studies Coordinator
Albuquerque Public Schools
Albuquerque, New Mexico

Dr. Mary A. McFarland
Instructional Coordinator of Social Studies,
 K-12 and Director of Staff Development
Parkway School District
Chesterfield, Missouri

Dr. Walter C. Parker
Associate Professor, College of Education
University of Washington
Seattle, Washington

CONTENT CONSULTANTS

Reading
Dr. Virginia Arnold
Senior Author, *Connections* Reading Program
Richmond, Virginia

Economics
Dr. George Dawson
Professor of Economics
Empire State University
Bellmore, New York

Special Populations
Dr. Jeanette Fleischner
Professor of Education
Teachers College
Columbia University
New York, New York

Multicultural
Jo Bonita Perez
Consultant
Los Angeles County Schools
Downey, California

Curriculum
John Sanford
Director of Curriculum
Acalanes Union High School District
Lafayette, California

Multicultural
Dr. Joe Trotter
Professor of History
Carnegie Mellon University
Pittsburgh, Pennsylvania

History
Dr. David Van Tassel
Founder of United States History Week
Professor of History
Case Western Reserve University
Cleveland, Ohio

Geography
Nancy Winter
Member of the Executive Board of the
 National Council for Geographic Education
Social Studies Teacher
Bedford, Massachusetts

International Education
Gary Yee
Principal
Hillcrest School
Oakland, California

GRADE-LEVEL CONSULTANTS

Monica Boylan Bonner
Elementary Teacher
Dr. Charles P. DeFuccio School
Jersey City, New Jersey

Rosemarie Heideman
First Grade Teacher
St. Agnes School
Ft. Wright, Kentucky

Marcia Kamstock
First Grade Teacher
Donna Klein Academy
Boca Raton, Florida

Tona Macken
First Grade Teacher
Ross Elementary School
Ross, California

Eleanor Mustaro
First Grade Teacher
St. Rose of Lima
New Haven, Connecticut

Diane K. Ringler
Elementary Teacher
Western Public School
Western, Nebraska

CONTRIBUTING WRITER

Loretta Kaim
Peekskill, New York

ACKNOWLEDGMENTS

The publisher gratefully acknowledges permission to reprint the following copyrighted material:
"Little Seeds" from THE WINDS THAT COME FROM FAR AWAY AND OTHER POEMS by Else Holmelund
Minarik. Copyright © 1964 by Else Holmelund Minarik. Reprinted by permisison of Harper & Row, Publishers, Inc.
"Big" from ALL TOGETHER by Dorothy Aldis, copyright 1925-1928, 1934, 1939, 1952, renewed 1953-1956,
1962, 1967 by Dorothy Aldis. Reprinted by permission of G.P. Putnam's Sons.

Macmillan/McGraw-Hill School Division
866 Third Avenue
New York, New York 10022

Printed in the United States of America
ISBN 0-02-145901-0
9 8 7 6 5 4 3 2 1

CONTENTS

UNIT 4 Our Country's History   128

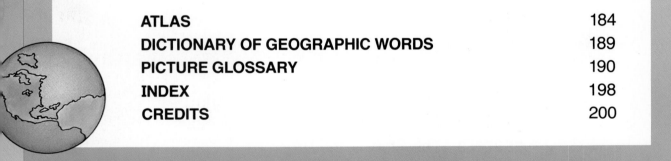

Charts and Graphs

Maps and Globes

USING YOUR TEXTBOOK

Your book has a **Table of Contents**.

The Table of Contents is at the front of your book.
It can help you find the things that are in your book.
Look for the Table of Contents.

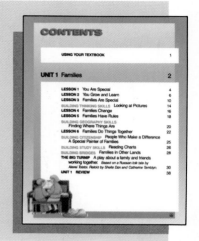

Your book has an **Atlas**.

The Atlas has some special maps.
You can use the maps in the Atlas as you learn about new places.
Use the Table of Contents to find the Atlas.

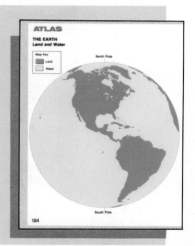

Your book has a **Picture Glossary**.

The Picture Glossary has pictures and sentences for all of the new words that you will learn.
Use the Table of Contents to find the Picture Glossary.

learn

family

Happy Birthday Grandma!

Our Jobs

	Do dishes	Set table	Take out garbage
Ned	X		
Mom	X		
Sue		X	
Dad			X

change

job

rule

You Are Special

This is Kim.

No one is just like Kim.

Kim is special.

The way Kim looks is special.

The things Kim likes
to do are special.

Kim's feelings are
special.

No one is just like you.
You are special, too!

In what ways are you special?

LESSON 2
You Grow and Learn

Once you were very little.
As time went by you grew.
You are still growing.

Steven at 3 months

Steven at 1 year

Steven at 6 years

As you grow you **learn**.

To learn is to find out new things.

You learned to walk and talk.

You learned to play games.

You learned to do many things.

This poem tells about growing and learning.

BIG

Now I can catch and throw a ball
And spell
Cat. Dog.
And Pig,
I have finished being small
And started
Being Big.

by Dorothy Aldis

Which things in the poem have you learned?

You are still learning.

You can learn from other people.

You can learn alone.

You can even help other
people learn.

Name three things that you have learned.

What can others learn from you?

Families Are Special

People who care about each other
are a **family**.
Families may be big or small.

How many people
are in these families?

11

Some people in a family live together
in the same place.
Some people in a family do not live together.

All families are special.

The people in a family make it special.

Who are the people that care about you?

Looking at Pictures

1. **LOOK** at the picture.

TELL who the people are.

14

Helping Yourself

To look means to see everything that is there.

One way to look at pictures is to:

- **CHOOSE** what to look for.
- **LOOK** to find everything about it.
- **TELL** all you see about it.

Do **CHOOSE**, **LOOK**, and **TELL** many times until you find out all you need to know.

2. There are five people in the picture.
Did you see a baby and a boy?
What other people did you see?

3. **LOOK** at the picture again.
TELL what the people are doing.

4. What can you do when you <u>look</u> at a picture?

4 Families Change

The people in families change.
Change means that things do not stay
the same.
The way people look changes with time.

In what ways has this
family changed?

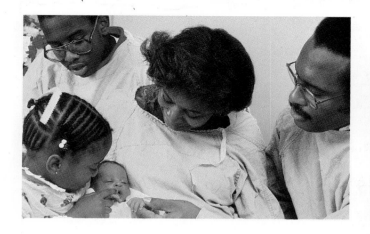

The number of people
in families can change.

Sometimes families change the place
where they live.

 Tell some other ways families can change.

Families Have Rules

All families have **rules**.

Some rules tell us what we should do.

Some rules tell us what we should not do.

Rules keep us from getting hurt.

Rules help us get
along with others.

 Tell some other rules families may have.
Why do families have rules?

Finding Where Things Are

These children are playing a game.

Read the game rules.

Game Rules

1. Play one at a time.
2. Take a tail.
3. Close or cover your eyes.
4. Turn around two times.
5. Try to put a tail on the **X** to win.
   If no one puts a tail on the **X**, the one who put a tail near the **X** wins.

Find where each of the children put a tail.

Ann put a tail <u>over</u> the donkey.

Ted put a tail <u>under</u> the donkey.

Eva put a tail to the <u>left</u> of the donkey.

Eddie put a tail to the <u>right</u> of the donkey.

Maria put a tail <u>far</u> from the donkey.

Ben just put a tail <u>near</u> the **X**.

Did any of the children put a tail <u>on</u> the **X**?

Who will win the game? Tell why.

Families Do Things Together

The people in families do things together.

They care about each other.

They take turns and share.

The people in families work together.
They help each other do jobs at home.
Any work is a job.
Working together can be fun.

The people in families play together, too.
Playing together can be fun.

Name some ways families can have fun.
Why do people in families do things together?

24

A Special Painter of Families

Anna Moses was so special that
everyone called her Grandma Moses.
Grandma Moses began to paint
when she was very old.
She liked to paint pictures of families
doing things together.
Many of her pictures are in museums
where all people can see them.
This is one of her pictures.
What is the family doing?

25

Reading Charts

Ana and Lou are holding a **chart**.
A chart can show many things.
Ana and Lou's chart shows the jobs that
they do at home.
Ana and Lou do the jobs that have a star.
What jobs does Ana do?
What jobs does Lou do?
What job do they both do?

Ana and Lou's Jobs

	Dust	Sweep	Water plants	Feed fish
Ana		★	★	
Lou	★	★		★

Garcia Family Jobs

	Set table	Feed Spot	Make bed	Cook
Mother			✓	✓
Pedro		✓	✓	
Grandpa		✓	✓	
Carmen	✓		✓	

This chart shows the jobs that the Garcia family does.

Use the chart to answer the questions.
1. What jobs does Pedro do?
2. What jobs does Carmen do?
3. What jobs does Grandpa do?
4. What jobs does Mother do?
5. What job do they all do?

Families in Other Lands

Families live in other lands.
Other lands are places like
Canada, Mexico, Nigeria, and Japan.

Canada

Mexico

28

Nigeria

Japan

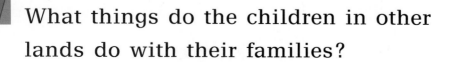 What things do the children in other
lands do with their families?

29

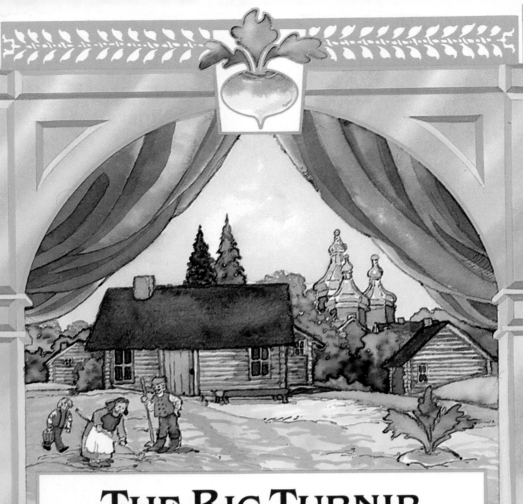

THE BIG TURNIP

Retold by Sheila Dori and Catherine Tamblyn

Have you ever heard of a turnip?
Well, Grandmother, Grandfather,
and their grandson, Troy, planted
one in their garden.
Over time, the turnip grew very big.
What do you think happened
when it grew too big?

The Players:

Grandmother

Troy

Grandfather

Dog

Cat

Storyteller

Pig

Mr. Goose

Mrs. Goose

Bird

(Grandmother walks into the garden.)

Grandmother: Our turnip has grown so big. I will pull it out to surprise Grandfather and Troy.

Storyteller: Grandmother pulled and pulled. But the big turnip did not move.

(*Grandmother walks out of the garden.*
Grandfather walks into the garden.)

Grandfather: I can't believe the size
of our turnip!
It has grown so big.
I will pull it out to surprise
Grandmother and Troy.

Storyteller: Grandfather pulled and pulled.
But the big turnip did not move.

Grandfather: Grandmother! Oh, Grandmother!
Please come and help me.
Let's pull the big turnip out together.

(*Grandmother walks into the garden.*)

Storyteller: Grandmother got behind
Grandfather.
They pulled and pulled.
But the big turnip did not move.

(Troy walks into the garden.)

Troy: Hi, Grandmother and Grandfather!
I will help you pull.

Storyteller: Troy got behind Grandmother.
Grandmother got behind Grandfather.
They pulled and pulled as hard as
they could.
But the big turnip did not move.

(The Dog and the Cat walk into the garden.)

The Dog: That turnip is so big!

The Cat: The Dog and I will help you pull.

Storyteller: The Cat got behind the Dog.
The Dog got behind Troy.
Troy got behind Grandmother.
Grandmother got behind Grandfather.

They all pulled and pulled.
And they pulled some more.
But the big turnip
did not move.

(Mr. Goose, Mrs. Goose, and the Pig walk into the garden.)

Mr. Goose: It looks like you need our help.

Mrs. Goose: We will help you pull.

The Pig: With our help, that big turnip will come out in a snap!

Storyteller: The Pig got behind Mrs. Goose.
Mrs. Goose got behind Mr. Goose.
Mr. Goose got behind the Cat.
They all pulled and pulled.
But the big turnip did not move.

Grandmother: Let's pull just one more time.

Grandfather: OK! Get ready. One . . . two . . . three . . . PULL!

(The Bird walks into the garden.)

Storyteller: As Grandfather cried "PULL!" the Bird pulled the Pig's tail.

The Pig: Ouch! Stop that!

The Bird: I'm helping, too!

Storyteller: All of a sudden there was a
loud sound.
The big turnip came out of the
ground so fast that they all
fell down!

Troy: I guess sometimes many helpers
have to work together to get
a job done.

Grandmother: Now that we've shared the
work, let's share a turnip dinner!

Words You Learned

Match each word with a picture.

| change | learn | family | rule | job | chart |

1.
	Feed Dog	Walk Dog	Wash Dog
Tim	✓		✓
Beth		✓	✓

2.

3.

4.

5.

6.

Ideas You Learned

1. Name two ways you have changed.
2. Name two people who help you learn.
3. Name one rule families have.
4. Name two jobs people in families do.
5. What things do people in families do together?

Building Skills

1. Reviewing Looking at Pictures

LOOK at the picture.

a. TELL all you can about the people.

b. TELL what the people are doing.

2. Reviewing Finding Where Things Are

Look at the picture.

a. Find the person on the <u>right</u>.

b. Find the person on the <u>left</u>.

c. Find what is <u>under</u> the table.

d. Find what is <u>over</u> the table.

e. Find what is <u>on</u> the table.

f. Find the person <u>near</u> the dog.

3. Reviewing Charts

Jobs Chart				
	Sweep Floors	Cook	Wash Clothes	Set Table
Mark	×			
Grandma			×	
Mother		×		
Ned				×

Use the chart to answer the questions.

a. What job does Grandma do?

b. What job does Mark do?

c. What job does Mother do?

d. Who sets the table?

Mommy   Nancy   Paul

Activities

1. Draw a picture of you doing something special.

2. Draw a picture of the people who care about you.
Name the people.

goods   needs   wants

A
Food

B
Toys
Games

42

clothes

Sid's
Shoes

Fall
Square
Dance
Saturday
October 30

season

weather

UNIT 2

Needs and Wants

Main Street

Marty's Store

shelter

service

People Have Needs

All people have **needs**.

Needs are things people must have to live.

People need food.

People need clothes.

44

People need a place to live.

People need love and care.

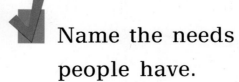 Name the needs
people have.

LESSON 2 People Need Food

People need food.

Food helps us to grow.

Food helps us to stay healthy.

People need to eat many kinds of food
to grow and to stay healthy.

46

How do people get the food they need?

Most people buy food in stores.

They buy food that other people grew or made.

Some people grow their own food.

Why do people need food?

Using Lists

Luke and his mother are at the store.
Luke made a **list** to help them shop.
The list will help them remember
the food they need to buy.
Read the list.
What food do they need?

Food we need to buy

bread
milk
apples
eggs
rice

Luke wants to make sure they have found
all of the food on the list.
What can he do to find out?
A good way to find out is to check the list.
Help Luke check the list.
Read the list again.
Look for each food.
Do they have all the food they need
to buy?
What food do they still need?

LESSON 3
People Need Clothes

People need clothes.

Some clothes are for work.

Other clothes are for play.

Clothes protect us from the weather.
The weather is what it is like outside.

Warm clothes are for cold weather.
Cool clothes are for hot weather.
Some clothes are for when it rains.
How do clothes for rain help us?

In some places, the weather changes as
the seasons change.

The seasons are
spring, summer,
fall, and winter.

Spring

Summer

52

Fall

Winter

Each season has different weather.
The people who live where the seasons
change need many kinds of clothes.

How do people get the clothes they need?
Most people buy clothes in stores.
They buy clothes that other people have made.

Some people make their own clothes.

Why do people need clothes?

What kinds of clothes do people need?

Finding What Is Alike and Different

1. **LOOK** at the things below.

TELL one way they are like each other.

Helping Yourself

One way to find how things are like each
other is to:

- **LOOK** at the first thing.

- **CHOOSE** something about it, such as
  its color, or how it is used.

- **LOOK** at the other things to see if they
  are like the first thing in the same way.

- **TELL** the way the things are like each
  other.

2. Things that are like each other are **alike**.
Things that are not alike are **different**.

The hat, the scarf, and the coat are
alike because they are all red and white.
In what other ways are they alike?
In what ways are they different?

3. **LOOK** at the things below.
TELL how they are alike.
TELL how they are different.

4. What can you do to find how things
are <u>alike</u> and <u>different</u>?

People Need Shelter

People need shelter.

A shelter is a place to live.

Homes are shelters.

Shelters protect people
from the weather.

They help keep people safe and warm.
Shelters give people a place to eat and sleep.

 Why do people need shelter?

Reading Addresses

Dan and his friend Rose live on Elm Street.
There are other houses on Elm
Street, too.
Each house has a number.
The number of a house and the name of
the street make up an **address**.

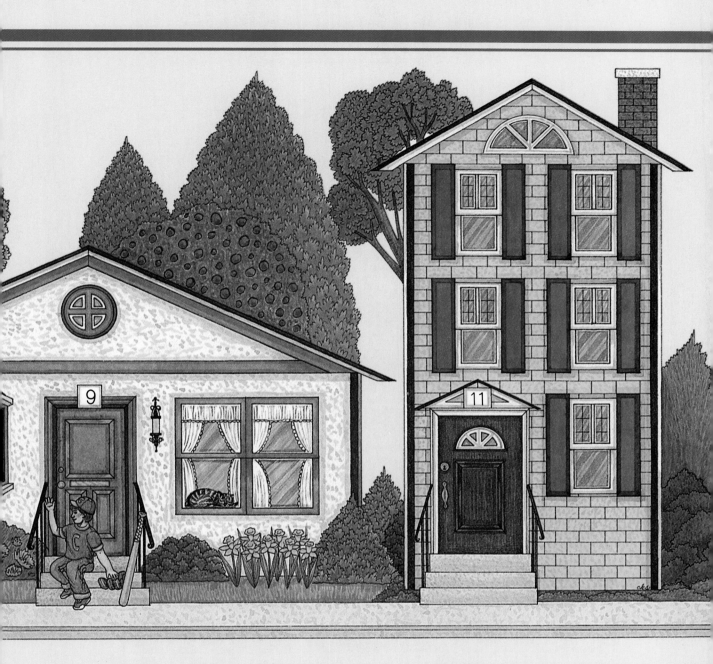

The address of Dan's house is 9 Elm Street.

Rose lives in the red house.

What is the address of Rose's house?

What is the address of the yellow house?

Using Floor Plans

This is Dan's house without a roof.
What things can you see in his house?

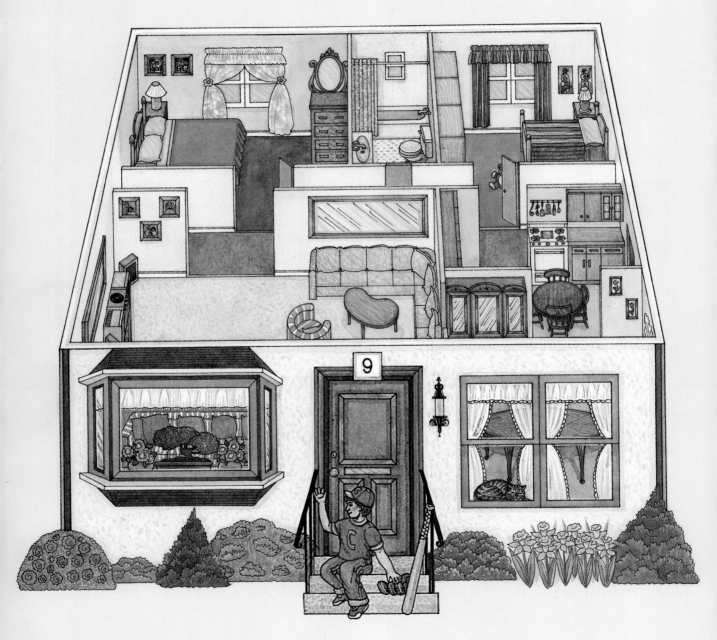

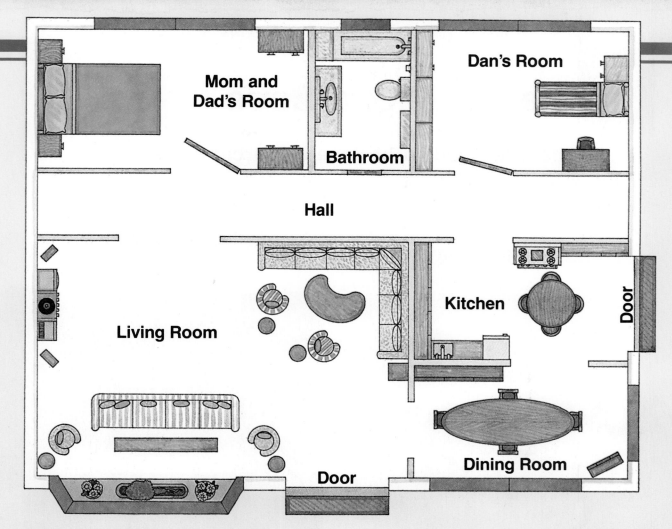

This drawing is a **map**.

A map is a drawing of a place.

This map is called a floor plan.

The floor plan shows all of the rooms in
Dan's house.

Use the floor plan to answer the questions.

1. What two rooms are next to the Living Room?

2. What room is next to Dan's Room?

3. What room is across from Mom and
Dad's Room?

63

People Need Love

People need to be loved and cared for.
People need to love and care for others.
People show love and care
in many ways.

Name two ways people care for others.

People Have Wants

People have needs.

People have **wants**.

Wants are things people would like to have.

Wants are things people can live without.

Which pictures show wants?

66

People cannot have everything they want.
They must choose the things they want most.

 How are wants different from needs?

Working for Needs and Wants

People use money to buy the things they need and want.

How do people get money?

People can earn money by working.

People work at different kinds of jobs.

Some people earn money by doing services.

Services are jobs people do for others.

69

Some people earn money by making or growing **goods** for others.

Goods are things that people use.

Some goods are things people need.

Other goods are things people want.

Children can earn money, too.
What other jobs can children do to
earn money?

Why do people work?

Needs and Wants in Other Lands

People in other lands have needs like you do.

They need food, clothes, shelter, and love.

People in other lands have wants, too.

Canada

Japan

Mexico

Nigeria

 What needs do people in other lands have?

The Little Red Hen

Retold by Catherine Tamblyn

This is a story about a Little Red Hen and her family of chicks.

The Little Red Hen works with her chicks to grow and make their own food.

Read the story to find out what they grow and what they make with it.

One day, the Little Red Hen found some grains of wheat.
The Little Red Hen said to her chicks,
"We can do something special with the grains of wheat.
I'll ask my friends to help."

The Little Red Hen asked her friends,
"Who will help me plant the grains?"
"Not I," said the cat.
"Not I," said the dog.
"Not I," said the duck.
"Then I will plant the grains,"
said the Little Red Hen.

The Little Red Hen and her chicks
made a big hole.
She planted the grains of wheat.
The grains grew and grew each day.
They grew into a tall wheat plant.

Soon the wheat was ripe and it
was ready to be cut.
The Little Red Hen asked her friends,
"Who will help me cut the wheat?"
"Not I," said the cat.
"Not I," said the dog.
"Not I," said the duck.
"Then I will cut the wheat,"
said the Little Red Hen.

The Little Red Hen cut
down the tall wheat plant.
Her chicks placed the
grains from the plant in a bag.
"Now the grains can be ground into flour
at the mill," said the Little Red Hen.

The Little Red Hen asked her friends,
"Who will help me take this bag
of grains to the mill?"
"Not I," said the cat.
"Not I," said the dog.
"Not I," said the duck.
"Then I will take it,"
said the Little Red Hen.

The Little Red Hen and her chicks took
the bag of grains to the mill.
Soon, the grains were ground into flour.

When they got back from the mill, the
Little Red Hen asked her friends, "Who
will help me make this flour into dough?"
"Not I," said the cat.
"Not I," said the dog.
"Not I," said the duck.
"Then I will make this flour into dough,"
said the Little Red Hen.

The Little Red Hen and her chicks
made the flour into dough.
The Little Red Hen put the dough into a
pan and said, "Now we are ready to bake."

The Little Red Hen asked her friends,
"Who will help me bake the bread?"

"Not I," said the cat.

"Not I," said the dog.

"Not I," said the duck.

"Then I will bake the bread,"
said the Little Red Hen.

The Little Red Hen put the pan
into a very hot oven.
Soon, she pulled a beautiful loaf of wheat
bread out of the oven.

The Little Red Hen asked her chicks,
"Who will help me eat some wheat bread?"
Just then, the cat called out, "I will!"
The dog called out, "I will!" and the
duck called out, "I will!"
"I don't think you should," said
the Little Red Hen.

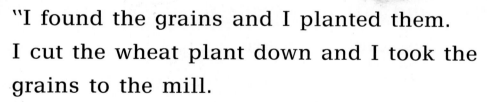

"I found the grains and I planted them.
I cut the wheat plant down and I took the
grains to the mill.
I made the dough and I baked the bread.
My chicks helped me with all the work,
so we should eat the bread!"

Who do you think should eat the bread?
Tell why.

Words You Learned

Use these words to finish the sentences.

needs	**shelters**	**weather**	**clothes**
wants	**seasons**	**services**	**goods**

1. Food, clothes, shelter, and love are _____.
2. Things that have been made or grown are _____.
3. A coat and a hat are warm _____.
4. People's homes are _____.
5. The four _____ are winter, spring, summer, and fall.
6. Games, toys, and bikes are _____.
7. Shelters protect people from the _____.
8. The jobs people do for others are _____.

Ideas You Learned

1. Name two ways people can get food.
2. Name two ways people can get clothes.
3. Why do people need to earn money?

Building Skills

1. Reviewing Lists

Help Mary check her list.
Draw a picture of
anything she still needs.

The things I have to buy
cheese
dog food
flowers
oranges
grapes

2. Reviewing Alike and Different

TELL how the things below are alike.
TELL how they are different.

3. Reviewing Addresses

Write an address for each house.

4. Reviewing Floor Plans

Use the floor plan to answer the questions.

a. What room is next to Dad's Room?

b. What two rooms are next to the Kitchen?

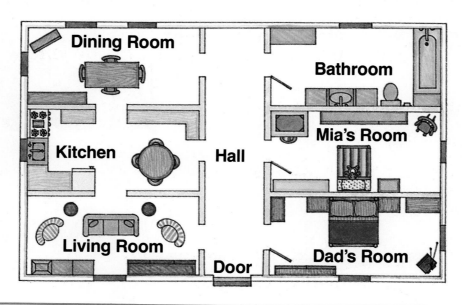

Activity

Read the poem "Little Seeds."

Draw four pictures to show the vegetable garden in each season.

Name your pictures Spring, Summer, Fall, and Winter.

LITTLE SEEDS

by Else Holmelund Minarik

Little seeds we sow in spring,
growing while the robins sing,
give us carrots, peas and beans,
tomatoes, pumpkins, squash and greens.

And we pick them,
one and all,
through the summer,
through the fall.

Winter comes, then spring, and then
little seeds we sow again.

peas

squash

carrots

state
Oregon
ocean

Map Key
water
land

United States of America

country

neighborhood   resource

earth

globe

north

west   east

south

UNIT 3

Places We Live

mountain

plain

river

neighbors

Places Where People Live

People live in many places.

Many people live in homes that are in
neighborhoods.

A neighborhood is a place where people
live, work, and play.

People who live near one another in a
neighborhood are **neighbors**.

This picture shows how a neighborhood
looks from an airplane.
What things can you see?

This is a map of the same neighborhood.

How is the map like the picture?

How is it different?

 What is a neighborhood?

Neighborhood Places

Neighborhoods are not all the same.
Some neighborhoods have only homes.
Some neighborhoods have homes
and other places.

Have you been to any neighborhood
places like these?
What did you do there?

 Name three neighborhood places.

Using Map Keys

Many maps have **symbols**.

Symbols stand for real things.

Symbols on a map are small pictures,

shapes, and colors.

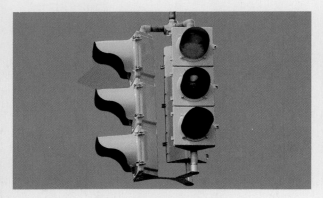 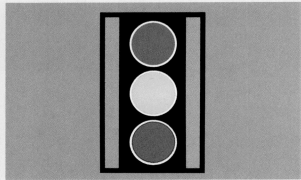

 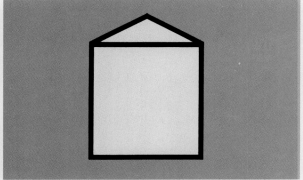

Maps that have symbols have a **map key**.

The map key tells what the symbols stand for.

The map on the next page shows Dan's neighborhood.

The map key will help you read the map.

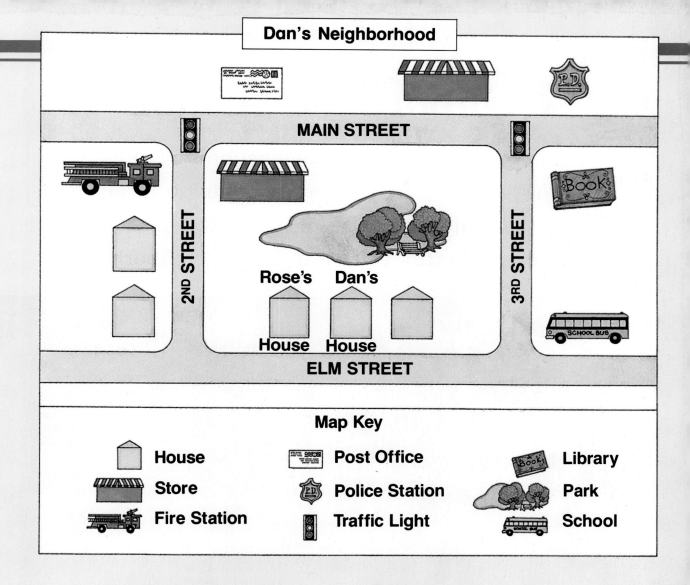

Dan's Neighborhood

MAIN STREET

2ND STREET

3RD STREET

Rose's   Dan's

House   House

ELM STREET

Map Key

House   Post Office   Library

Store   Police Station   Park

Fire Station   Traffic Light   School

Use the map and the map key to answer
the questions.

1. What symbol stands for the Library?
2. What symbol stands for the Post Office?
3. What symbol stands for the School?
4. How many Houses are there in Dan's neighborhood?
5. How many Traffic Lights are there in
   Dan's neighborhood?

3 Neighborhood Schools

Some neighborhoods have schools.

A school is a place where people go to learn.

These children are as old as you.

They go to this school in their neighborhood.

Our School

Map Key

■ classrooms
  our classroom
■ Principal's Office
■ Hall
■ Nurse's Office
■ Library
● Gymnasium
🍎 Cafeteria
🎨 Art Room

The children made this map.

What does their map show?

In what ways is their school like yours?

Why do people go to school?

Knowing School Rules

Schools have rules.

Rules in schools help us get along
with others.

Sometimes there are problems when people
do not know the rules.

Miguel is waiting for a drink.

Amy pushes in front of him.

What rules should Amy know? Why?

Scott is telling a story.

Sarah and Jack keep talking.

What rules should Sarah and Jack know? Why?

The fire bell is ringing.

Barry and Lisa are running to the door.

What rules should Barry and Lisa know? Why?

Reading a Neighborhood Map

Our Neighborhood Walk

1. We started on Elm Street in front of the <u>School</u>.

2. We walked past the <u>Park</u>.

3. We saw the <u>Library</u> on our right.

4. We walked past the <u>Meat Store</u> and the <u>Toy Store</u>.

5. We mailed a letter at the <u>Post Office</u> before we walked past the <u>Fire Station</u>.

6. We walked past <u>Rose's House</u> and <u>Dan's House</u> on our way back to the <u>School</u>.

Dan's class at school took a walk around his neighborhood.
Read the chalkboard in the picture.
It tells the way Dan's class walked.
Look at the map on the next page.

100

Find the place where Dan's class started.
Then move your finger on the map to find
the way Dan's class walked.

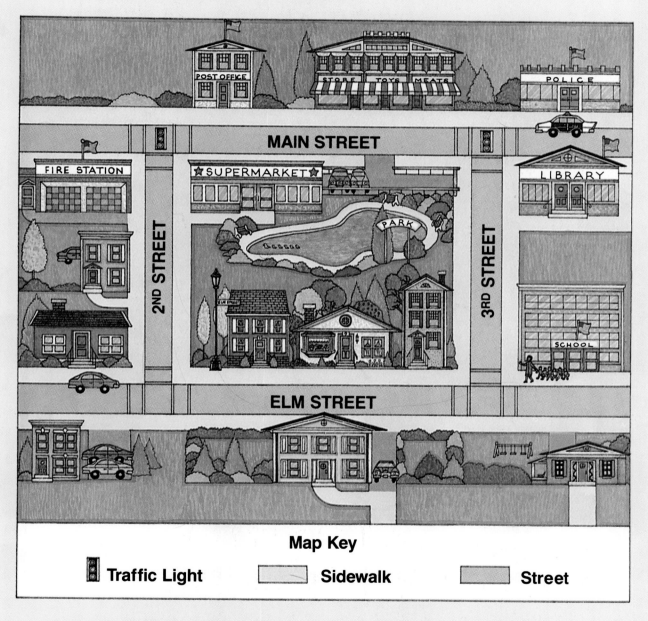

Name the streets that Dan's class walked along.

Neighborhoods Change

Neighborhoods change with time.
This picture shows a neighborhood long ago.
What things do you see?

This picture shows the same neighborhood
as it looks today.
What things do you see?
In what ways has the neighborhood changed?

 Name one way a neighborhood can change.

Sorting Things into Groups

1. SORT the things below into two groups.

Helping Yourself

To sort means to place together things that are alike.

One way to sort things is to:

- **LOOK** at one thing.
- **FIND** another thing that is like it.
- **NAME** how the two things are alike.
- **FIND** all the things that are like these and place them together.

2. You may have placed the shelters
in a group named Homes.
What is a good name for the other group?

3. **FIND** the things below that are alike.
SORT them into groups.

4. When can <u>sorting things into groups</u> help you?

Living in the United States

All of the neighborhoods that you have learned
about are alike in a very special way.
They are neighborhoods in a place called
the United States of America.

All of the people you have
learned about are alike, too.
They are all Americans.
They live in the
United States of America.

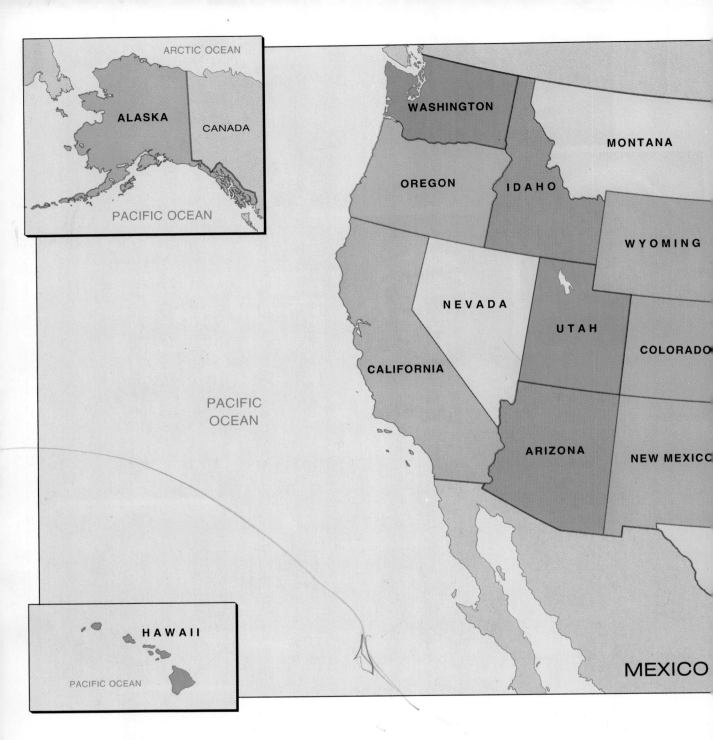

This is a map of the United States of America.

The United States is a country.

A country is a land and the people who live there.

The United States is a country with 50 states.

CANADA

NORTH DAKOTA
MINNESOTA
SOUTH DAKOTA
WISCONSIN
MICHIGAN
MAINE
VERMONT
NEW HAMPSHIRE
NEW YORK
MASSACHUSETTS
RHODE ISLAND
CONNECTICUT
PENNSYLVANIA
NEW JERSEY
NEBRASKA
IOWA
ILLINOIS
INDIANA
OHIO
DELAWARE
MARYLAND
WEST VIRGINIA
VIRGINIA
KANSAS
MISSOURI
KENTUCKY
NORTH CAROLINA
OKLAHOMA
ARKANSAS
TENNESSEE
SOUTH CAROLINA
ATLANTIC OCEAN
MISSISSIPPI
GEORGIA
ALABAMA
TEXAS
LOUISIANA
FLORIDA
Gulf of Mexico

THE UNITED STATES OF AMERICA

Each state is a part of the United States.

Each state has a different name.

Americans live in each state.

What state do you live in?

109

Each state has a different size and shape.

This is a map of the state of Tennessee.

Tennessee has a long and thin shape.

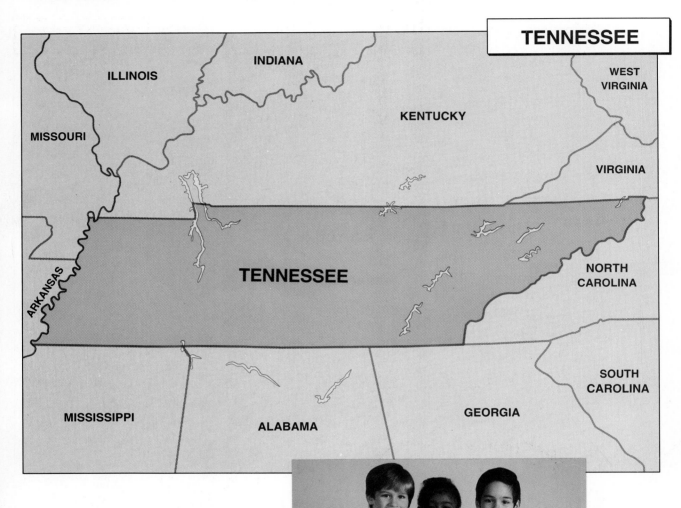

These Americans
live in Tennessee.

Oklahoma has the shape of a pan.
People call Oklahoma the "Panhandle" state
because of its special shape.

These Americans
live in Oklahoma.

What country do Americans live in?
What are Tennessee and Oklahoma?

111

The United States is a beautiful country. The many kinds of land and water help to make our country beautiful.

The United States has a kind of land called **plains**.
Plains are very flat land.

The United States has high land called hills.

The United States even has **mountains**.

Mountains are the highest kind of land.

The United States has many kinds of water.

A **river** is a body of water.

Rivers flow across the land.

Three **oceans** are near parts of the United States.
An ocean is a very big body of salt water.
The Atlantic, the Pacific, and the Arctic
oceans are near the United States.

Name the kinds of land and water that
make our country beautiful.

Our Country's Resources

The United States has many resources.
Resources are things from nature that people use.

Wood

Gas

Water

Soil

All Americans must try to take care
of our country's resources.
Resources need to last a long time.

 Name a resource that you use.

Living on the Earth

This is a picture of the earth in space.
The earth is the place where all people live.
The earth has land and water.
The United States is part of the land
on the earth.

This is a **globe**.
A globe is a model of the earth.
A globe is round like the earth.
A globe shows land and water.
The United States is part of the
land shown on a globe.

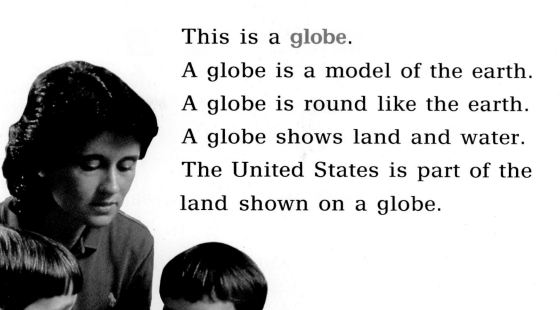

Tell how the globe is like the earth.
Tell how the globe is different from
the earth.

Reading Directions

There are four **directions** on the earth.
Directions are north, east, south, and west.
Directions can help you tell where places are.

North is the direction toward the North Pole.
Find the North Pole.
South is the direction toward the South Pole.
Find the South Pole.
When you face north, east is to your right.
When you face north, west is to your left.

Find North America and South America.

1. Tell why North America is called
   North America.
2. Tell why South America is called
   South America.
3. Is the United States a part of North
   America or South America?

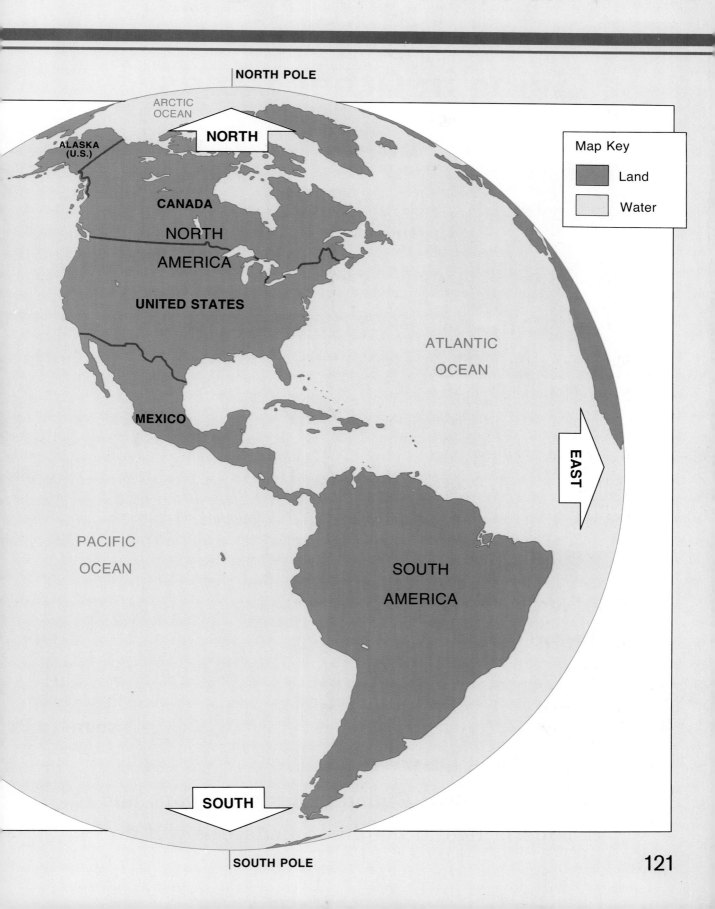

NORTH POLE

ARCTIC
OCEAN

NORTH

ALASKA
(U.S.)

CANADA

NORTH
AMERICA

UNITED STATES

MEXICO

ATLANTIC
OCEAN

EAST

PACIFIC
OCEAN

SOUTH
AMERICA

Map Key

Land

Water

SOUTH

SOUTH POLE

121

Living in Other Lands

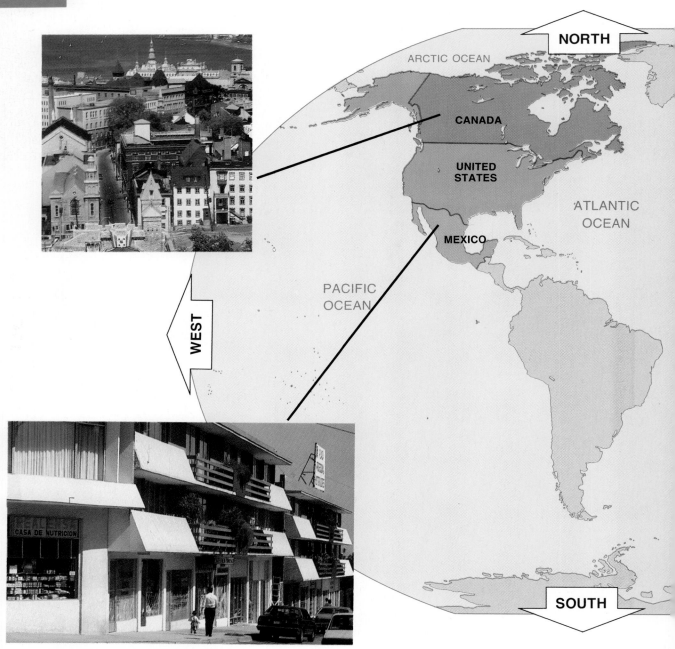

The people in Canada, Mexico, Japan, and Nigeria live in neighborhoods like you do.

They also live in a country like you do, because these lands are countries, too!

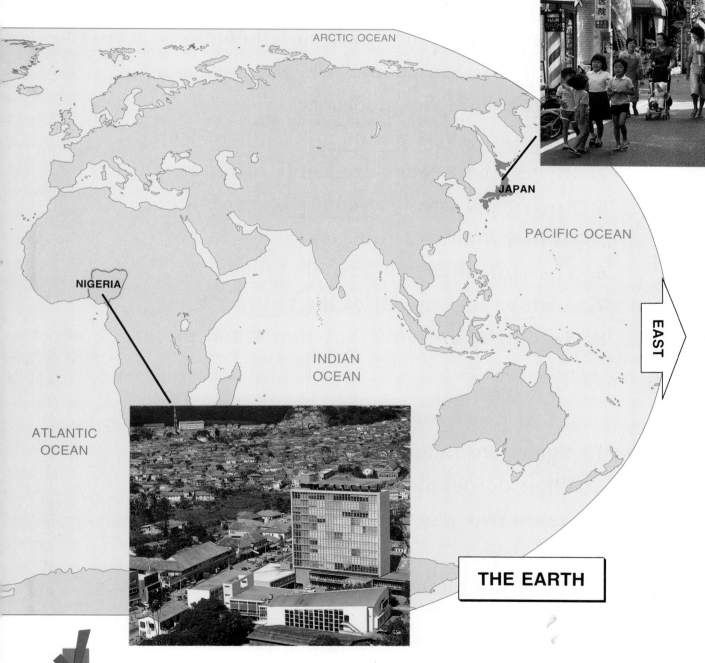

ARCTIC OCEAN

JAPAN

PACIFIC OCEAN

NIGERIA

INDIAN OCEAN

EAST

ATLANTIC OCEAN

THE EARTH

Name two ways in which the people in other lands are like you.

Words You Learned

Tell if the sentences are true or false.

1. All <u>neighborhoods</u> have only homes.

2. <u>Neighbors</u> are people who live near one another in a neighborhood.

3. <u>Mountains</u> and <u>plains</u> are kinds of water.

4. <u>Rivers</u> and <u>oceans</u> are kinds of land.

5. Americans live in a <u>country</u> called the United States of America.

6. The United States has 50 <u>states</u>.

7. A <u>globe</u> is a model of the <u>earth</u>.

8. <u>Resources</u> are drawings that stand for real things.

Ideas You Learned

1. Name two neighborhood places. What do people do at these places?

2. Name two ways a globe and the earth are alike.

3. Write the names of your country and your state.

4. Name two ways people use the resource water.

Building Skills

1. Reviewing Map Keys and Neighborhood Maps

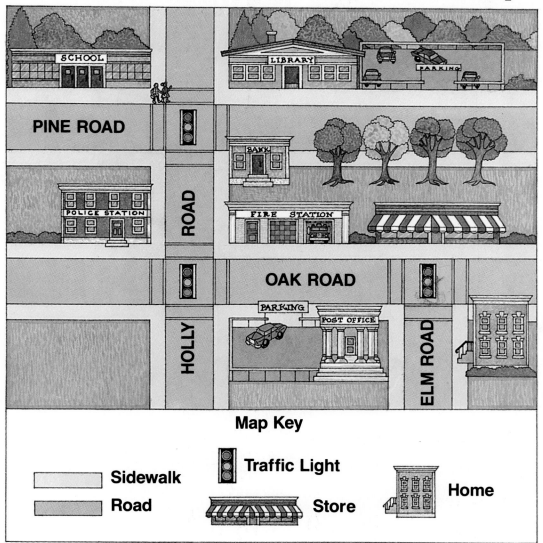

Sam and Tina are walking Home from School.

They both live in the Home on Elm Road.

Tell what roads they will walk along.

Tell what places they will walk past.

2. Reviewing Directions

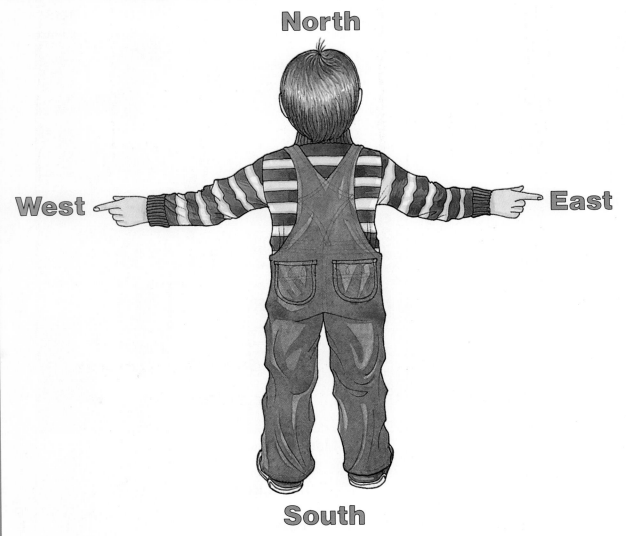

Use the picture to answer the questions.

If you face north, what direction is behind you?

What direction is to your right?

What direction is to your left?

3. Reviewing Sorting Things into Groups

FIND the things below that are alike.

SORT them into groups.

Activity

Many neighborhoods have signs with symbols.

Match each sign with what it stands for.

NOVEMBER 24TH

THANKSGIVING DAY PARADE

holiday

Happy Thanksgiving

tepee

hide

Christopher Columbus

The Sioux

history

Indians

128

American flag

UNIT

4

Our Country's History

The Pilgrims

The Story of the First Americans

North

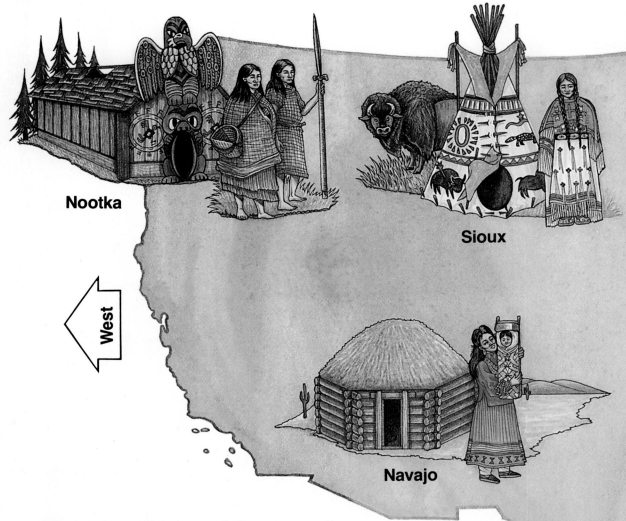

Nootka

Sioux

West

Navajo

South

Our country and its people
have changed with time.
The story that tells what our country
was like long ago is our history.
The story of the first Americans is
part of our country's history.

The first Americans were Indians.
There were many Indian groups.
Indians lived in many parts
of America.

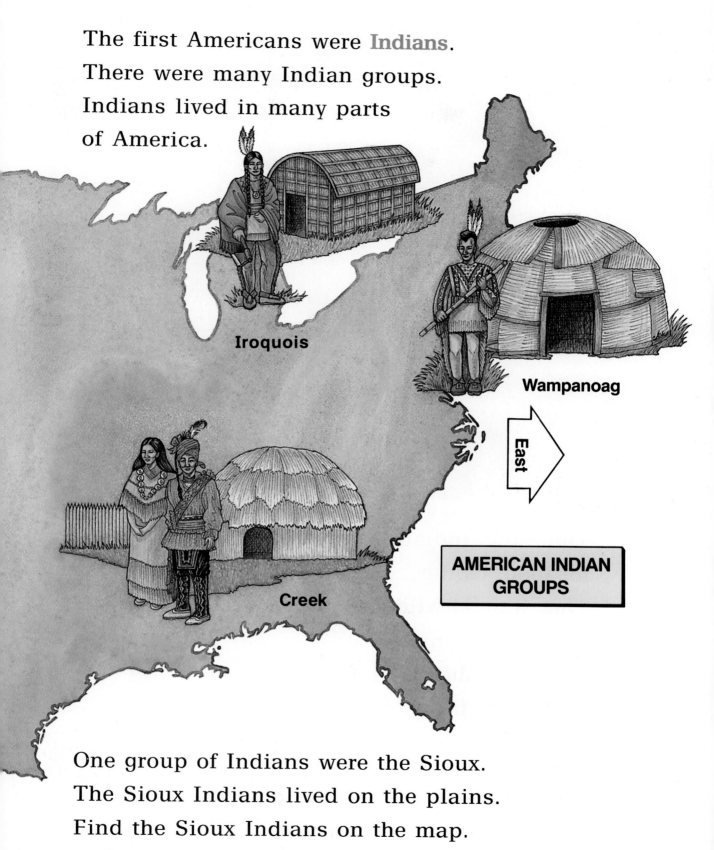

Iroquois

Wampanoag

East

AMERICAN INDIAN
GROUPS

Creek

One group of Indians were the Sioux.
The Sioux Indians lived on the plains.
Find the Sioux Indians on the map.

The Sioux Indians met their own needs
for food, clothes, and shelter.
They hunted wild animals like the buffalo
for food and hides.
Hides are the skins of animals.
The Sioux Indians made their clothes
from hides.

They even made their tepees from hides.
A tepee is a shelter made with wood poles
and hides.
The Sioux Indians liked to paint symbols
on their tepees.
The symbols told a story.

What needs did the Sioux Indians have?
How did they meet their needs?

The Story of Christopher Columbus

Long ago, some Indians in another part of America saw something that they had never seen before.

At first, the Indians may have thought they saw three great white birds on the Atlantic Ocean. What they really saw were three ships named the *Niña,* the *Pinta,* and the *Santa Maria.*

Christopher Columbus was the captain of the
Santa Maria.

He and his crew had come across the Atlantic
Ocean from a country called Spain.

They were looking for new lands.

The new land that Columbus came to was America.

Soon many people from other lands came to
America to live.

To what new land did
Christopher Columbus come?

The Story of the Pilgrims

Many people from other lands came to America to live.

One group of people were the Pilgrims.

The Pilgrims came to America from England on a ship named the *Mayflower.*

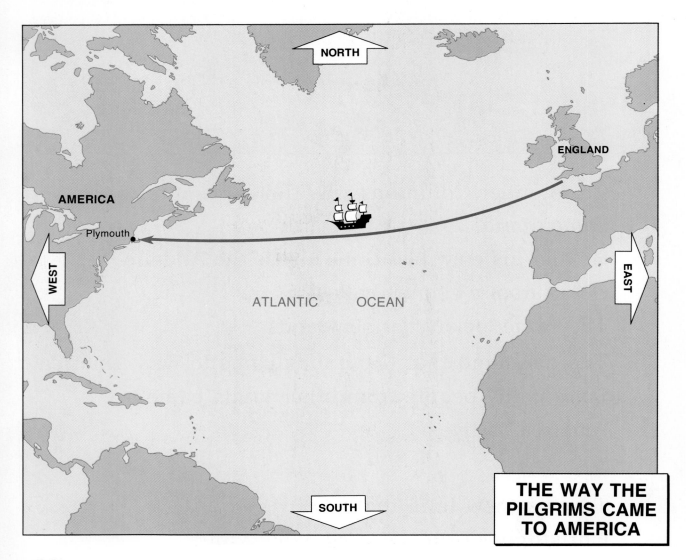

NORTH

ENGLAND

AMERICA

Plymouth

WEST

EAST

ATLANTIC   OCEAN

SOUTH

THE WAY THE PILGRIMS CAME TO AMERICA

The Pilgrims had a very hard time at first.
It was winter when they got to America.
They had no shelters to keep them warm, and
they had only a little food left to eat.
The Pilgrims made huts to live in, and they
shared food over the long, cold winter.

When spring came, the Pilgrims made
better homes.
Some Indians helped the Pilgrims hunt and
fish for food.
They even helped the Pilgrims plant and
grow food.

When fall came, the Pilgrims had lots of food.
They made a special dinner called a feast.
They asked the Indians to share it with them.

This was the first Thanksgiving.
The Pilgrims gave thanks to God for
the food they had to eat.
They gave thanks for the help the Indians
had given them.
They gave thanks for their new home
in America.

 In what ways did the Indians help
the Pilgrims?

139

Putting Things in Order

1. **LOOK** at the pictures.

TELL what comes first, next, and last
to make a story.

Helping Yourself

One way to tell what comes first, next,
and last is to:

- **LOOK** at each picture.
- **TELL** all you can about each picture.
- **FIND** the picture that comes first.
- **FIND** the picture that comes next.
- **FIND** the picture that comes last.

2. When you told what picture came first, next, and last, you put them in **order**.

First, the Pilgrim planted the corn.
Next, the Pilgrim picked the corn.
Last, the Pilgrim cooked the corn.

3. **LOOK** at the pictures.

PUT them in order to tell a story.

4. What should you do when you <u>put</u> <u>things</u> <u>in</u> <u>order</u>?

LESSON 4 Our Country's Holidays

Our country has many holidays.
A holiday is a special day.

You learned about the first Thanksgiving.
Thanksgiving is now a holiday for
all Americans.
Like the Pilgrims, Americans give thanks for
many things on Thanksgiving.

142

Let's sing a special Thanksgiving song.

Over the River and Through the Wood

Traditional Melody
Words by Lydia Maria Childs

1. O - ver the riv - er and through the wood,
2. O - ver the riv - er and through the wood,

To grand - moth - er's house we go; _____
Trot fast _____ my dap - ple gray! _____

The horse knows the way to car - ry the sleigh
Spring o - ver the ground like a hunt - ing hound, _

Through the white and drift - ed snow.
_ For this is Thanks - giv - ing day!

143

Independence Day is another holiday.

It is our country's birthday.

On Independence Day, we think about how the United States of America became a country long ago.

Many holidays are for special people in our country's history.

Columbus Day is a holiday, too.

On Columbus Day, we think about Christopher Columbus and how he came to America.

Some holidays are for special things.

Arbor Day is a special day for trees.

Many Americans plant trees on Arbor Day.

They show how much they care about trees.

Name one holiday.

Tell why it is a special day.

A Special Person Who Loved Trees

John Chapman lived in our country long ago.

John loved trees.

Everywhere John went, he gave apple seeds to people for planting.

Soon, beautiful apple trees grew in many parts of our country.

There were lots of good apples to eat, too!

John Chapman planted so many apple seeds that people named him Johnny Appleseed.

147

Learning the Days of the Week

Every week has seven days.

Each day has a different name.

The days of the week are always in the
same order.

Sunday is the first day of the week.

These children are planning for a special day.

Look at their plan on the next page.

What does their plan show?

The children will follow the plan each day.

What will the children do on Thursday?

What time will they do it?

What will they do on Monday?

What time will they do it?

Our Plan For The Week

Days of the Week	Things We Will Do	Times We Will Do Things
1. Sunday	No School	
2. Monday	Learn Indian Symbols  sun	
3. Tuesday	Make Indian Drums 	
4. Wednesday	Make Indian Headdresses 	
5. Thursday	Make Indian Necklaces 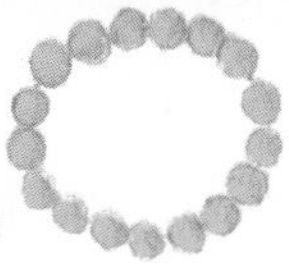	
6. Friday	Learn Indian Signs 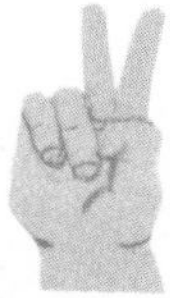 friend	
7. Saturday	American Indian Day! Walk in Parade	

What day is the parade?

What time does it start?

Learning Months and the Calendar

A year has 12 **months**.

Each month has a different name.

The months of the year are always in the same order.

January is the first month of the year.

What is the last month?

What month is before June?

What month is after August?

In what month is your birthday?

A **calendar** is a special chart.

This calendar is for the month of July.

Each block on the calendar is a day.

Each day has a number.

JULY

Sunday	Monday	Tuesday	Wednesday	Thursday	Friday	Saturday
	1	2	3	4 Independence Day	5	6
7	8	9	10	11	12	13
14	15	16	17	18	19	20
21	22	23	24	25	26	27
28	29	30	31			

All months do not have the same number of days.

How many days are in this month?

What holiday is on July 4?

Why is the holiday special for Americans?

Our Country's Symbols

You know that symbols stand for things.
There are many symbols that stand for
our country.

The American flag is a symbol of our country.
The American flag is red, white, and blue.
It has 50 stars.
Each star stands for a state.

I pledge allegiance to the flag
of the United States of America,
and to the Republic for which it stands,
one Nation under God, indivisible, with
liberty and justice for all.

Many Americans say the
Pledge of Allegiance to
our flag each day.

Name a place where you say the
Pledge of Allegiance to our flag.

These symbols stand for our country, too.

Bald Eagle

Liberty Bell

Statue of Liberty

The White House

 Tell three things about the American flag.

Name two other symbols of our country.

155

Words You Learned

Use these words to finish the sentences.

history	holiday	tepees
Indians	hides	American flag

1. The _____ is a symbol of our country.

2. A _____ is a special day.

3. The first Americans were _____.

4. The Sioux Indians made clothes from _____.

5. The Sioux Indians lived in _____.

6. The story that tells what our country was like long ago is our _____.

Ideas You Learned

1. What three things did the Pilgrims give thanks for?

2. Name two of our country's holidays. Tell why they are special days.

3. Tell all you can about the American flag. Name two places where you have seen our flag.

Building Skills

1. Reviewing Putting Things in Order

LOOK at the pictures.

PUT them in order to tell a story about the Pilgrims coming to America.

2. Reviewing Days of the Week

What day comes next?

a. Sunday Monday ___?___

b. Wednesday Thursday ___?___

c. Saturday Sunday ___?___

3. Reviewing Months

What month comes next?

a. January February ___?___

b. April May ___?___

c. July August ___?___

d. October November ___?___

4. Reviewing Calendars

Use the calendar to answer the questions.

a. What month does the calendar show?

b. How many days are in the month?

c. What holiday is in the month? Why is the holiday special for Americans?

Activity

Long ago, the Sioux Indians painted picture symbols like these on their tepees.
Draw a tepee.
Then draw symbols on it like the Sioux Indians did.

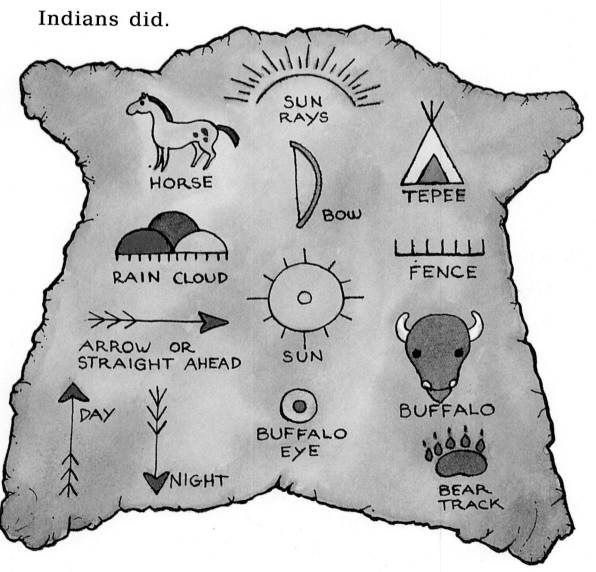

| George Washington | Betsy Ross | Abraham Lincoln |
| **President** | | **President** |

law

All children have the right to go to school together.

Martin Luther King, Jr.

George Washington

There were many special Americans in our country's history.
They helped to make our country great.
George Washington was a very special American.

George Washington helped to start our country
long ago.

He was our country's first President.

The President is the head of our country.

Americans call George Washington
the "Father of Our Country."

The Granger Collection

Presidents' Day is a holiday in February.
We think about George Washington on this day.
You may see cherries on Presidents' Day.
Read the story to find out why.

GEORGE WASHINGTON
AND
THE CHERRY TREE

Some people say this story did not happen.
But Americans like to tell it because it is
about ideas we believe in.

When George Washington
was six years old,
he cut down his father's
cherry tree.

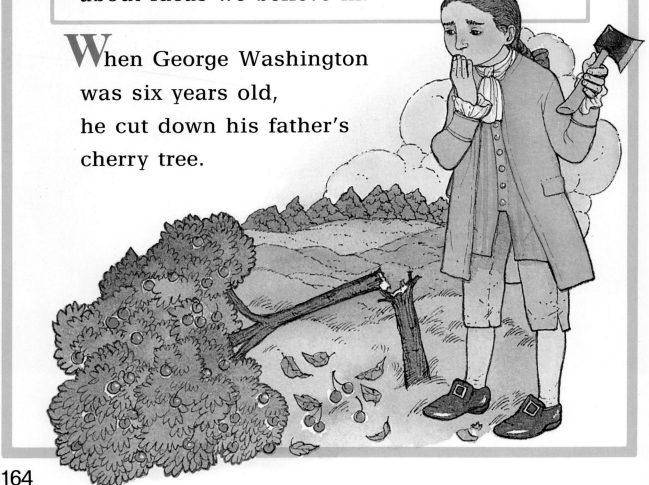

George's father was not very happy
when he saw his tree.
"George," called his father.
"Do you know who cut down my
cherry tree?"

George said, "I cannot tell a lie, Pa.
You know I cannot tell a lie.
I did cut it with my hatchet."
George's father did not punish him.
He was happy that George had
told the truth.

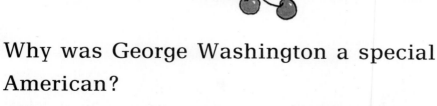

Why was George Washington a special
American?
Why do Americans like to tell the
cherry tree story?

2 Betsy Ross

Betsy Ross was a special American.
Some people say she made the first
American flag.
The flag was the first symbol of our country.
In what ways is her flag like the American
flag today?
In what ways is it different?

Flag Day is June 14.

On Flag Day, we think about Betsy Ross.

We think about the American flag and what it stands for.

What did Betsy Ross do for our country?

What does the American flag stand for?

Abraham Lincoln

Abraham Lincoln was a special American
who people called "Honest Abe."
He was President a long time after
George Washington.

Abraham Lincoln helped to make more of the
people in our country free.

Presidents' Day is a holiday when we also
think about Abraham Lincoln.
On this day, we think about how he helped to
make our country the land of the free.

Why was Abraham Lincoln a special American?

Predicting

1. **READ** the story.

TELL what will happen next.

An Abe Lincoln Story

1 When Abe Lincoln was a boy, he worked in a store.

2 One day, a woman bought some cloth from him.

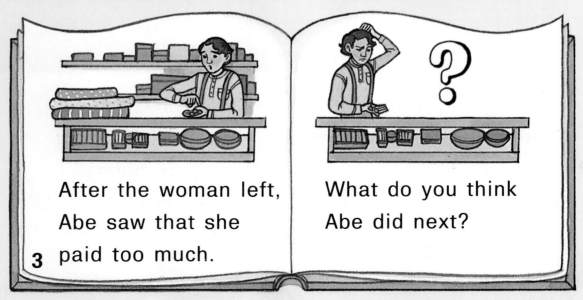

3 After the woman left, Abe saw that she paid too much.

What do you think Abe did next?

2. Abe Lincoln could have kept the money.
What other things could he have done?
This is what really happened.

After the woman left, Abe saw that she paid 3 too much.

Abe walked very far to give the woman back her money. 4

3. PREDICT what could happen next.
4. What should you do when you <u>predict</u>?

Martin Luther King, Jr.

Martin Luther King, Jr., was a
special American.

He wanted **laws** that were fair for
all Americans.

Laws are rules that all people must follow.

He wanted all Americans to
get along together.

Martin Luther King Day is in January.
On this holiday, we think about how Martin
Luther King, Jr., worked to make our laws
fair for everyone.

Why was Martin Luther King, Jr.,
a special American?

Reading Pictographs

Carla and Robert found some books about
Martin Luther King, Jr., in the library.
They made a **pictograph** to show the
number of books they found.
A pictograph is a graph that uses pictures
to show how many things.

Special American	Books We Found 📖 = 1 Book
Martin Luther King, Jr.	📖 📖 📖

Each picture on Carla and Robert's
pictograph stands for one book.
Count the pictures on the pictograph.
How many books did they find in the library
about Martin Luther King, Jr.?

174

Special Americans	Books Found	= 1 Book
George Washington		
Betsy Ross		
Abraham Lincoln		
Martin Luther King, Jr.		

Use the pictograph to answer the questions.

1. What does each picture stand for?
2. How many books are about Betsy Ross?
3. How many books are about Abraham Lincoln?
4. Are there more books about Abraham Lincoln or George Washington?
5. Are there more books about Martin Luther King, Jr., or Betsy Ross?

You Can Be a Special American

The United States is a great country.
Its people have helped to make it great.

You can help to keep our country great.

You can follow rules and our country's laws.

You can help other Americans.
You can show others that you care
about our country.

You can help to keep
our country's land
and water beautiful.

You can help to take care
of our country's resources.

GLASS

NEWS
PAPERS

You can make a difference.

You can be a special American, too!

Let's sing this song about our country.

America

My coun-try 'tis of thee, Sweet land of lib - er - ty,

Of thee I sing. Land where my fa - thers died, Land of the

Pil-grim's pride, From ev - 'ry _ moun-tain-side Let _ free-dom ring.

Name two things you can do to be a special American.

Words You Learned

Use these words to finish the sentences.

| laws   pictograph   President   predict |

1. The _____ is the head of our country.
2. A _____ is a graph that uses pictures to show how many things.
3. Rules that everyone must follow are _____.
4. When you _____ you tell what will happen next.

Ideas You Learned

1. What special American was our country's first President?
2. What special American wanted our country to be the land of the free?
3. What symbol did Betsy Ross make?
4. What was one thing Martin Luther King, Jr., wanted?
5. Name two ways you can help other Americans.

Building Skills

1. Reviewing Predicting

When Abraham Lincoln was a boy,
people could only walk or use horses to
go from place to place.

Over time there have been many
changes in the ways people can go from
place to place.

THINK about all the ways people can go
from place to place.

PREDICT how people might go from
place to place when you grow up.

2. Reviewing Pictographs

Helpers	Cans We Filled		= 1 Can	
Jane	🗑	🗑	🗑	🗑
Paul	🗑	🗑		
Juan	🗑	🗑	🗑	
Beth	🗑	🗑		

How are these children being good Americans?

Use the pictograph to answer the questions.

a. What does the pictograph show?

b. What does one picture stand for?

c. How many cans did Juan fill?

d. What helper filled the most cans?

e. How many cans were filled in all?

Activity

Use the chart to answer the questions about George Washington and Abraham Lincoln when they were your age.

History Facts	George Washington	Abraham Lincoln
State	Virginia	Kentucky
Kind of home	farm house	log cabin
Schoolwork they liked the best	5+3=8 2+7=9 arithmetic	Aesop's Fables reading
Things they did for fun	ride a horse	read a book

1. Who lived in the state of Virginia?

2. In what kind of home did Abraham Lincoln live?

3. What did Abraham Lincoln like to do for fun?

4. Who liked the schoolwork called arithmetic?

ATLAS

THE EARTH
Land and Water

Map Key

Land

Water

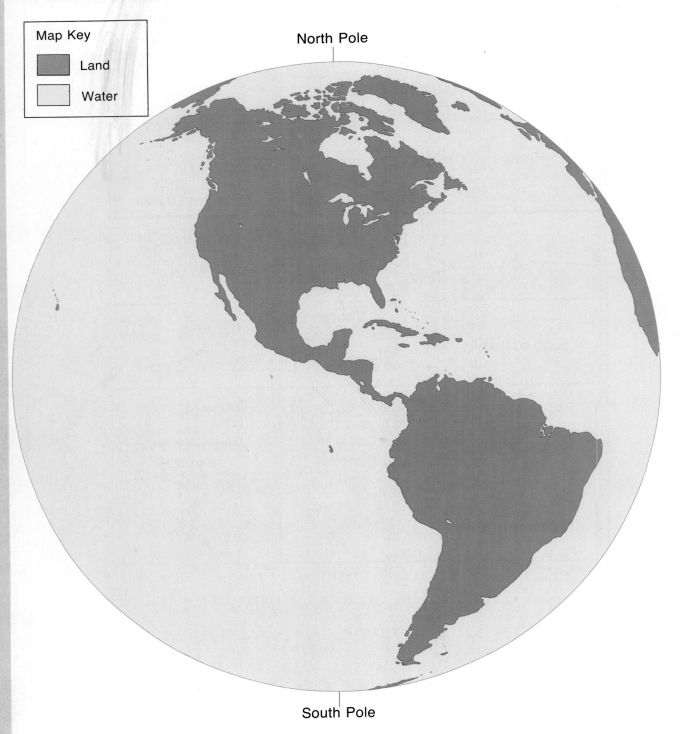

North Pole

South Pole

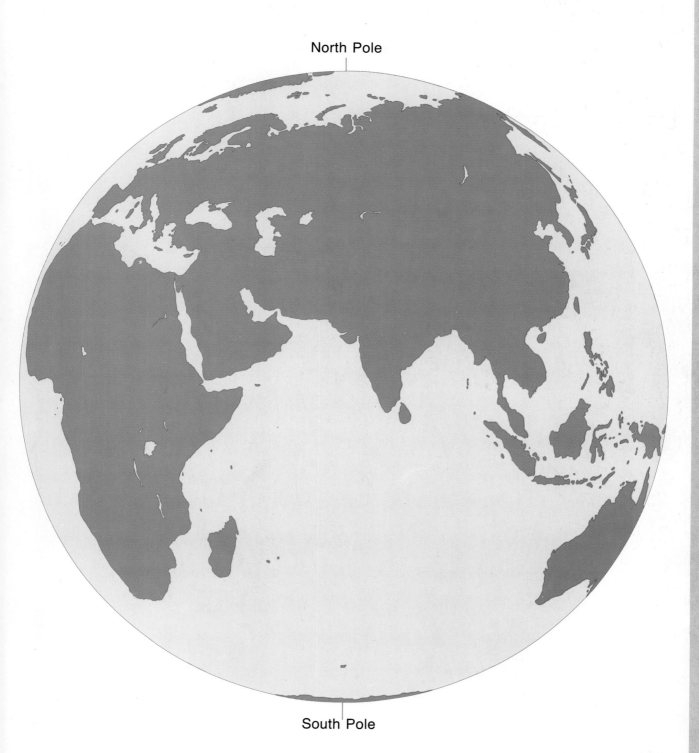

North Pole

South Pole

185

NORTH

WEST

SOUTH

ARCTIC OCEAN

ALASKA

CANADA

PACIFIC OCEAN

WASHINGTON

MONTANA

OREGON

IDAHO

WYOMING

NEVADA

UTAH

COLORADO

CALIFORNIA

ARIZONA

NEW MEXICO

PACIFIC
OCEAN

MEXICO

HAWAII

PACIFIC OCEAN

CANADA

NORTH DAKOTA

MINNESOTA

Lake Superior

MAINE

VERMONT

NEW HAMPSHIRE

SOUTH DAKOTA

WISCONSIN

MICHIGAN

Lake Huron

NEW YORK

MASSACHUSETTS

RHODE ISLAND

CONNECTICUT

NEBRASKA

IOWA

Lake Michigan

Lake Erie

Lake Ontario

PENNSYLVANIA

NEW JERSEY

ILLINOIS

INDIANA

OHIO

Washington, D.C.✹

DELAWARE

MARYLAND

WEST VIRGINIA

VIRGINIA

KANSAS

MISSOURI

KENTUCKY

EAST

OKLAHOMA

ARKANSAS

TENNESSEE

NORTH CAROLINA

SOUTH CAROLINA

MISSISSIPPI

ALABAMA

GEORGIA

TEXAS

LOUISIANA

ATLANTIC OCEAN

FLORIDA

Gulf of Mexico

THE UNITED STATES OF AMERICA

Map Key

✹ National capital

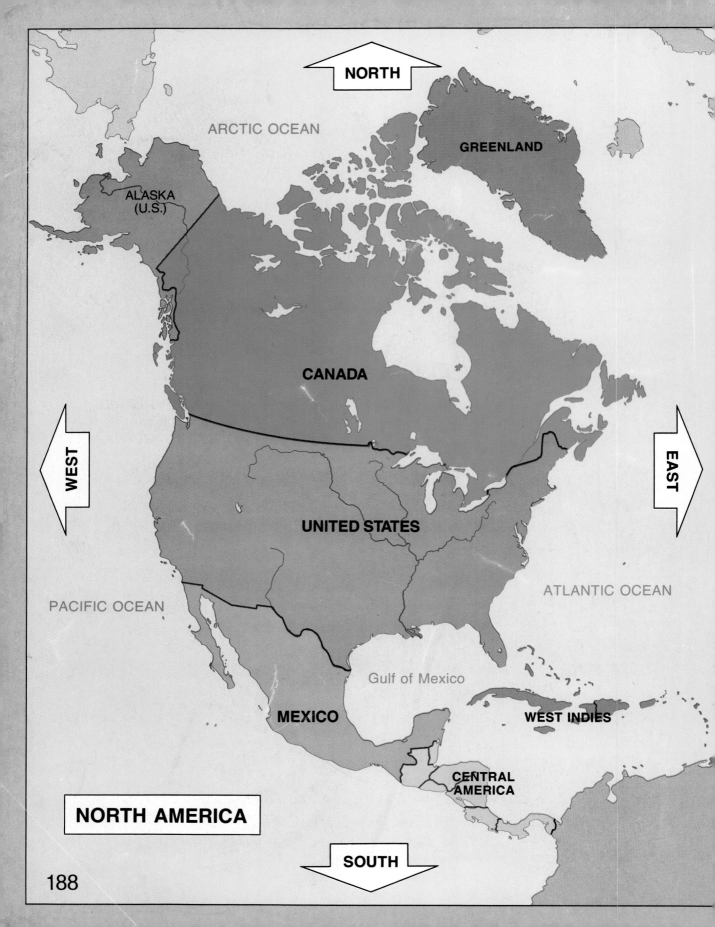

NORTH

ARCTIC OCEAN

GREENLAND

ALASKA
(U.S.)

WEST

EAST

CANADA

PACIFIC OCEAN

UNITED STATES

ATLANTIC OCEAN

Gulf of Mexico

MEXICO

WEST INDIES

CENTRAL
AMERICA

NORTH AMERICA

SOUTH

DICTIONARY OF
GEOGRAPHIC WORDS

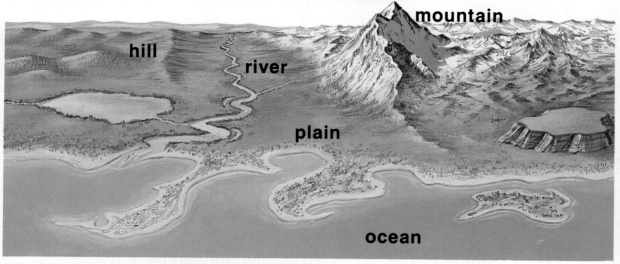

mountain

hill

river

plain

ocean

hill
A **hill** is land that is raised, but is lower than a mountain.

mountain
A **mountain** is the highest kind of land.

ocean
An **ocean** is a very big body of salt water.

plain
A **plain** is very flat land.

river
A **river** is a body of water that flows across the land.

189

PICTURE GLOSSARY

address
My **address** is
62 Parker Road. (page 60)

alike
My mittens are **alike**.
(page 57)

American flag
The **American flag** is red,
white, and blue. (page 152)

calendar
This **calendar** shows the
month of July. (page 151)

	JULY					
Sunday	Monday	Tuesday	Wednesday	Thursday	Friday	Saturday
1	2	3	4	5	6	7
8	9	10	11	12	13	14
15	16	17	18	19	20	21
22	23	24	25	26	27	28
29	30	31				

change
I **change** as I grow. (page 16)

chart
Our **chart** shows the things we like to do. (page 26)

clothes
I wear warm **clothes** when the weather is cold. (page 50)

country
Our **country** is the United States of America. (page 108)

different
My shoes are **different** from Karen's shoes. (page 57)

directions
North, east, south, and west are **directions**. (page 120)

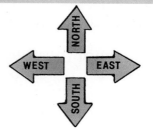

earth
The **earth** has land and water. (page 118)

family
My family likes to
work together. (page 10)

globe
I can find our country
on a globe. (page 119)

goods
My wagon, my shoes, and this apple
are goods. (page 70)

hide
The Sioux Indians made their
clothes from hides. (page 132)

history
The story of the Pilgrims
is history. (page 130)

holiday
Independence Day is a holiday.
(page 142)

Indian

The **Indians** were the first Americans. (page 131)

job

My **job** is to water the plants. (page 23)

law

Our country has **laws** that we must follow. (page 172)

learn

My teacher helps me to **learn** to swim. (page 7)

list

We use a **list** to help us shop. (page 48)

map

This **map** shows some neighborhood places. (page 63)

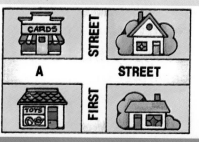

map key

A **map key** helps me read a map. (page 94)

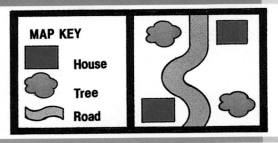

month

January is the first **month** of the year. (page 150)

mountain

The **mountain** has snow on it. (page 113)

needs

Our **needs** are food, clothes, shelter, and love. (page 44)

neighbor

Jenny is my **neighbor**. (page 89)

neighborhood

My **neighborhood** has houses and other places. (page 89)

ocean
We play near the **ocean**.
(page 115)

order
I can write numbers in **order**.
(page 141)

pictograph
This **pictograph** shows how
many fish we have. (page 174)

FISH WE HAVE	🐟 = 1 FISH
MARK	🐟🐟🐟🐟🐟
SALLY	🐟🐟🐟

plain
The farmers grow wheat
on the **plain**. (page 112)

predict
I **predict** that it will rain soon.
(page 171)

President
George Washington was our
country's first **President**. (page 163)

PICTURE GLOSSARY

resource
Trees are a **resource** that people use.   (page 116)

river
I saw boats on the **river**.
(page 114)

rule
One **rule** I follow is to go to bed at 8 o'clock.   (page 18)

season
Fall is a **season**.
(page 52)

service
My barber does a **service** when he cuts my hair.   (page 69)

shelter
A home is a **shelter**.   (page 58)

state

Arizona is a **state** in the United States.
(page 108)

symbol

This picture **symbol** stands for a tree. (page 94)

tepee

A **tepee** is a shelter made from hides. (page 133)

wants

Toys and games are **wants**. (page 66)

weather

Rain and snow are kinds of **weather**. (page 51)

INDEX

CREDITS

200